MATHmatazz
Activity Guide

Kindergarten

Scott Foresman
Addison Wesley

http://www.sf.aw.com   http://www.ctw.org

EDITORIAL
For CTW
Publisher: Nina B. Link • Vice President, School Products: Laurie Weisman • Vice President, School Marketing: MaryEllen McLaughlin • Project Manager: Kristine Tania Malferrari • Director of Research: William Yotive • Writer/Coordinating Editor: Tracey West • Interior Design: Béatrice Schafroth • Writers, Puppet Plays and Games: Lalie Harcourt and Ricki Wortzman • Copy Editor: Anthony Sacramone • Proofreader: Margaret Mittelbach • Advisor: Joel Schneider, Ph. D.

For Scott Foresman – Addison Wesley
Program Authors: Lalie Harcourt and Ricki Wortzman • Consulting Project Manager: Cindy Greene

ART CREDITS
Cover: Richard Kolding; page 7: Kristen Mathieu; page 8: Peter Panas; page 9: Ron Zalme; pages 10-11: Jessica Wolk-Stanley; page 13: Ron Zalme; pages 14-15: Jessica Wolk-Stanley; page 17: Richard Kolding; page 18: Kristen Mathieu; page 19: Donna Reynolds; page 21: Andrew Shiff; pages 22-24: Ron Zalme; Game boards: Kristen Mathieu

PHOTO CREDITS
pages 1, 4-6, 12, 16, 20: Kevin McDevitt

Copyright © Addison Wesley Longman, Inc. and Children's Television Workshop

All rights reserved. You are hereby granted the right to duplicate pages 10-11, 14-15, and 22-24 of this book and game-board directions and playing pieces for classroom use. Otherwise, the publication is protected by Copyright, and permission should be obtained from the publisher prior to any prohibited reproduction, storage in a retrieval system, or transmission in any form or by any means, electronic, mechanical, photocopying, recording, or otherwise. For information regarding permission, write to Scott Foresman - Addison Wesley, Permissions Department, 1900 East Lake Ave., Glenview, Illinois 60025.

MATHmatazz™ is a trademark of Addison Wesley Longman, Inc. and Children's Television Workshop.

 is a trademark of Children's Television Workshop.
http://www.ctw.org
Printed in the United States of America.

ISBN: 0-201-31754-0

3 4 5 6 7 8 9 10 BX 01 00 99 98

Table of Contents

Chapter	Key Concepts	
Welcome to MATHmatazz	A description of the MATHmatazz components	4
1 **Video:** The Block Party	Attributes; sorting; using location vocabulary such as *in, out, over, under,* and *between*	6
2 **Game:** What Will Herman Wear?	Sorting by shape, color, and size	7
3 **Book:** Red Blocks, Blue Blocks	Using attributes to make patterns; understanding that there is more than one way to make a pattern	8
4 **Puppet Skit:** Step by Step	Counting from 1-5; understanding number order	9
5 **Video:** Herman's Surprise	Counting from 0-10 and back again	12
6 **Puppet Skit:** Riddle With Herman	Measurement; using vocabulary such as *longer than* and *shorter than*	13
7 **Video:** Shapes for Sale	Shapes; solids; recognizing and naming the shapes in solids such as cones, boxes, cylinders, pyramids, and rectangular prisms	16
8 **Book:** Animal Trouble	Number sense; counting from 1-10; understanding ways to make numbers to 10	17
9 **Game:** Story Time	Time; money; sequencing	18
10 **Book:** Bugs, Slugs, and Butterflies	Joining and separating groups	19
11 **Video:** The Super-Duper Art Show	Ordering and comparing numbers from 0-31; skip counting by 5s	20
12 **Book:** The Mixed-Up Collection	Addition and subtraction up to 10	21
Reproducibles	Puppet and mask templates to photocopy and use with the puppet plays	22

Welcome to MATHmatazz

Dear Teacher, in this Activity Guide you'll find support for using all of your MATHmatazz components. There is a motivating MATHmatazz video, book, game, or puppet skit to use with every chapter in Scott Foresman – Addison Wesley MATH. Use MATHmatazz to introduce chapters, to reinforce concepts in the middle of a chapter, and/or to review concepts at the end of a chapter. Students will enjoy using these components over and over again. The MATHmatazz components have been designed especially for Scott Foresman – Addison Wesley MATH by Children's Television Workshop, creators of *Sesame Street, The Electric Company, Ghostwriter, 3-2-1 Contact, Square One TV, Big Bag,* and other top-quality educational programs. They are guaranteed to help you put the smile back in math.

Annie and Herman are two best friends who use and think about math in the same way that your students do. Annie (right) is a lovable 5-year-old girl who loves adventure and is a creative problem solver. Herman (left) is a hermit crab who loves shapes, counting, patterns, and riddles. They will be your students' guides in all of the MATHmatazz videos, books, games, and puppet plays described in this Activity Guide.

Using the Components

The Videos

Annie and Herman use math as they sing, dance, and play their way through four mathematical adventures. Each video includes a song. Learning these songs will help students remember key mathematical ideas. Here are some tips for making the most of the videotapes.

- Use the videotapes several times during the course of a chapter: to introduce a concept, reinforce it, and to review it at the end.
- Whenever possible, preview videos before showing them to your class.
- Before showing the tape, use the Before Viewing questions to establish a context.
- Use the pause and rewind buttons on your videotape player to allow students to make predictions, discuss ideas, and review information during viewing.
- To help you, we've included a brand-new interactive feature called PAWS. When you see the 🐾, one of the characters will pose a question. The picture will freeze for about 15 seconds. Pause your videotape player to allow students time to discuss answers. When you release the pause button, a musical cue will let you know the story is resuming. The characters will then answer the questions.
- After viewing a tape all the way through, discuss it, and then view it again. Pause when necessary to clarify a concept presented on screen.
- Encourage students to sing along with the songs. Rewind to review the songs so that students can learn them.

The Books

Four read-aloud storybooks present Annie and Herman using math in a variety of situations.

- Questions are posed throughout the stories. Encourage students to discuss their answers before turning the page.
- At the end of each book you'll find a series of extension activities.
- Use the Before Reading questions to set the scene before you read.

The Puppet Skits

Your students can take on the roles of Annie and Herman and star in math productions right in your classroom! In this Activity Guide you'll find scripts and instructions for puppet plays that support Chapter 4 and Chapter 6. The plays were written to involve the whole class in the math concept. Reproducible templates for stick puppets and masks are provided in the back of this guide.

The Games

Games are ideal for practicing math skills. Use these toward the middle or end of a chapter to practice new math skills. You'll find game boards in the pocket in the back of this Activity Guide. You'll find reproducible rule sheets and playing pieces on the back of each game board. For ideas on using the games with your students, see pages 7 and 18 in this Activity Guide.

CHAPTER 1: The Block Party

Key Concepts

- Using attributes of color and texture to identify objects

- Using the words *in, out, over, under,* and *between* to identify position and location

About the Video

One of Annie's blocks is missing! She finds the missing block, and she also finds something even better — a lovable hermit crab named Herman. To welcome her new friend to the neighborhood, Annie throws him a block party!

Approximate running time: 16 minutes

Before Viewing

- Tell the class they will be meeting two new friends, Annie and Herman. Ask what they know about hermit crabs and explain they'll be meeting a hermit crab in a few minutes.

- Ask: *What is a block party?* A block party is usually an outdoor party where everyone on the block is invited. In this story students will attend a different kind of block party.

- Ask whether students have ever found a toy or something else that they liked and weren't sure who it belonged to. What did they do? Discuss their ideas about what to do in such a situation. Tell them that something similar is going to happen in the upcoming story.

- Let students know they'll be asked to work in pairs after viewing to retell the story to each other. Retelling gives students a chance to develop their vocabulary and understanding of the story in a non-threatening situation. Use this activity with all of the videotapes.

- See page 5 for more tips on using the videotape.

The Song

In the song "The Block Party," your students will review the concepts of *over, under,* and *between.*

Extending the Video

- After watching the video, divide the class into small groups. Provide each group with a collection of blocks, counters, or cubes of various sizes, shapes, and colors. Challenge each group to sort its blocks in a number of different ways and to give a reason for its actions.

- Organize a block hunt. While students are out of the classroom for lunch or another activity, hide as many blocks as there are students in different areas of the room. Have students search until they each find one block. Encourage each student to describe where the block was found by using the vocabulary of position and location (*I found it under the desk; I found it in the drawer*).

CHAPTER 2

What Will Herman Wear?

Key Concepts

- Recognizing the attributes of shape, color, and size

- Matching objects according to attributes

- Sorting objects according to attributes

About the Game

Children will have fun helping Herman to decide what to wear as they try to fill in shapes on one of four shells. The first completed shell is the one Herman will wear.

Before Playing

- Discuss the shells on the game board with students. Ask: *What is the same about all of the shapes in this shell? In this one? How are the shapes in this shell different?*

- Introduce and discuss the procedure for selecting and sorting the shapes. Hold up a game piece and ask students to identify its attributes: *What size is it? What shape? What color?*

- Use this cooperative game for 1-3 players to reinforce concepts in Chapter 2.

- See page 5 for more tips on using the game.

Preparation

- Remove the game board from the pocket in the back of this activity guide.

- On the back of the game board, you'll find a reproducible rule sheet as well as reproducible playing pieces. Duplicate, color, and cut the shapes from the back of the game board. You may wish to laminate them for greater durability.

Extending the Game

- Have children design their own shells for Herman by using crayons and paper. Ask them to identify their sorting rule.

- The child who puts the final piece on Herman's shell uses this rhyme to describe the shell according to a sorting rule: *Herman is a handsome crab. The shell with all of the _____ (child fills in sorting rule) is the one he will grab.*

Activity Guide ★ MATHmatazz 7

CHAPTER 3

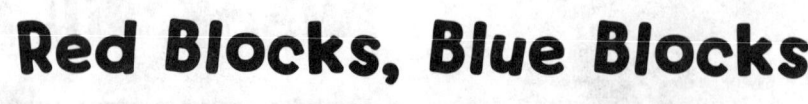

Red Blocks, Blue Blocks

Book

Key Concepts

- Sorting items according to color, shape, and function

- Making patterns

- Understanding that there is more than one way to make a pattern

About the Book

Annie's tree house is a mess! Annie and Herman have got to clean it up. Leave it to Annie to make their chore fun. She and Herman arrange everything into patterns!

Before Reading

- Ask students: *What is a pattern?* Record their ideas. Explain that this is a book about patterns.

- Ask students to look at the book cover. *How have Annie and Herman arranged the blocks between them?* Explain that the alternating red and blue blocks form a pattern.

- Ask students to tell a partner what they think might happen in this story.

- Let students know that you'll be asking them to retell the story to each other in pairs after you've read it. Retelling the story helps children work on comprehension, sequencing, and vocabulary. Telling it to a partner is easier than addressing the whole class.

- See page 5 for more tips on using the book.

Extending the Book

- To strengthen both language arts and math skills, put students in pairs or small groups, and ask students to retell the story to one another using words or pictures. If you wish, let students use their Annie and Herman puppets or masks (pp. 22–24).

- Return to your list of students' ideas about patterns to see if they want to add anything.

- Practice auditory patterns by clapping in different patterns.

- Turn to the back of the book for more extension activities.

Step by Step
Puppet Skit

About the Puppet Skit

There are so many things to build with blocks. Today, Herman is in the mood to build steps. With Annie's help, he'll keep adding blocks until his steps are done.

Key Concepts

- Developing number relationships from 1-5
- Understanding number order

Before Performing

- Photocopy the puppets and masks on pages 22-24.
- Organize the props and choose volunteers to play Annie and Herman as described on the next page. Give each volunteer a puppet.
- Copy these counting chants onto chart paper. Point to them as the children chant the rhymes together. Chanting these portions with a distinctive beat helps to accentuate the counting sequence.
- See page 5 for more tips on using the puppet skit.

First Chant:
1
1, 2
1, 2, 3!

Second Chant:
1
1, 2
1, 2, 3
1, 2, 3, 4!

All we did is add 1 more!

Third and Final Chant:
1
1, 2
1, 2, 3
1, 2, 3, 4
1, 2, 3, 4, 5!

Counting makes us feel alive!

Extending the Skit

- Retell the skit, and have the children in the audience build their own set of steps as the skit progresses.
- This skit ends with a question that naturally leads to further investigation. Children can use connecting cubes to build a set of steps that extend beyond 5. Encourage the children to describe the steps in relationship to one another. For example, 4 and 1 more is 5, 5 and 1 more is 6, 6 is 1 more than 5, 5 is 1 more than 4, and so on.

Activity Guide ★ MATHmatazz 9

Step by Step
Puppet Skit Script

As the skit begins, Herman is at the front of the classroom with six cubes arranged as steps of 1, 2, and 3 cubes. Annie is nearby, and the teacher is off to one side. 9 loose cubes are on a desk nearby.

Props
- a puppet for each child
- one stack each of 1, 2, and 3 connecting cubes
- 9 loose cubes

Characters

Herman and Annie: Choose two children to play Herman and Annie. They don't have speaking roles but will respond to your narration. As children become comfortable with the play, prompt Annie and Herman to speak their own lines.

Teacher: You will narrate the script and also prompt the characters. (An older student or assistant could be recruited to prompt the characters.)

☞ This symbol points to italicized text, which will help you prompt students to follow along with the action.

Teacher: You all know how Annie and Herman love to collect things. Well, they also love to build. One day Herman decided to build with his collection of blocks. He wanted to build a set of steps. He thought that a good set of steps would come in handy for reaching high things.

☞ *Prompt Annie to move over to Herman.*

Teacher: When Annie came over, Herman was already counting the blocks in his steps.

☞ *Instruct Annie to join Herman.*

Teacher: Let's help Herman count!

☞ *Point out the first chant on the chart paper, and read it through once. Then encourage all students to lift their puppets and move them to the beat as they join the chant.*

1,
1, 2
1, 2, 3!
(repeat)

Teacher: Annie was very excited. Counting and building are two of her very favorite things to do. She quickly joined the fun. "Let's dance, Herman!" Annie said.

☞ *Prompt students to join in the chant again; have them move their puppets in time with the beat.*

Annie,	1
Herman,	1, 2
and Class:	1, 2, 3!

(repeat)

Teacher: When Annie and Herman stopped dancing, they took a deep breath. "Let's add another step," Herman said. How many blocks do you think they

	needed for the next step? *(Class should reply, "4")*
Teacher:	To students who responded "4": **How did you decide that 4 is the next step?** *(Accept reasonable replies.)*
☞	*Prompt Annie and Herman to go to the pile of loose blocks.*
Teacher:	**Herman and Annie ran over to the loose pile of blocks, and each took 2 back to the steps. They joined the 4 blocks and then counted to see if 4 really was right.**
☞	*Prompt Herman and Annie to go to the loose pile and make a step out of 4 blocks. Lead students in the second chant:*
Annie,	1
Herman,	1, 2
and Class:	1, 2, 3!
	1, 2, 3, 4!
	All we did is add 1 more! *(repeat)*

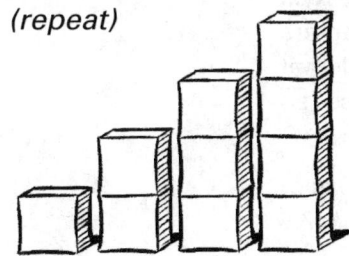

Teacher:	**Annie and Herman decided that adding one more to each set of steps was a good idea. They decided to make another step. How many blocks do they need?** *(Class should reply, "5")*
Teacher:	To students who responded "5": **How did you decide that 5 is the next step?** *(Accept reasonable replies.)*
☞	*Prompt Annie and Herman to go to the pile of loose blocks.*
Teacher:	**Annie and Herman ran over to the pile and got 5 more blocks. They joined them together and added them to the staircase.**
☞	*Prompt Herman and Annie and helpers to make a new step with 5 blocks and add it to the other steps.*
Teacher:	**Herman and Annie sang and danced as they counted their last step.**
☞	*Lead children in the third counting rhyme, instructing them again to move their puppets in time to the chant.*
Annie,	1
Herman,	1, 2
and Class:	1, 2, 3!
	1, 2, 3, 4
	1, 2, 3, 4, 5!
	Counting makes us feel alive! *(repeat)*
Teacher:	**Herman and Annie thought the new steps were beautiful. Annie wanted to make more. But Herman said they were out of blocks. Then Annie had an idea. "Let's go on a block hunt!" she said. Herman thought that was a great idea. "Annie, you're the best friend a crab could have!" he said.**
☞	*Prompt Herman and Annie to leave the set.*
Teacher:	**So Annie and Herman went block hunting. How many blocks do you think Annie and Herman need to find to make their next step?**
☞	*Encourage children to respond and explain their ideas.*

CHAPTER 5

Herman's Surprise

Key Concepts

- Counting from 1-10

- Counting from 10 all the way back to 0

About the Video

Annie's got a special treat for her friend Herman. She's built an elevator so that Herman can visit the tree house. Herman is so happy that he prepares a surprise for Annie—10 beautiful rocks. There's only one problem—10 rocks are too heavy for the tree house elevator. Students will have fun counting to 10 and back again as Herman tries to figure out a way to give Annie his surprise.

Approximate running time: 18 minutes

Before Viewing

- The title of this story is "Herman's Surprise." Ask students what a surprise is. What do they think Herman's surprise might be?

- Ask: *Who can count forward and backward from 1 to 10?* Let volunteers demonstrate what they know.

- Let students know there will be times when the characters will need their help and that the videotape will pause so they can answer questions.

- Ask: *What is more: 10 rocks or 5 rocks? 4 rocks or 5 rocks? 9 rocks or 10 rocks?*

- See page 5 for more tips on using the videotape.

Extending the Video

- In the video Herman gives Annie 10 rocks, and Annie gives Herman 10 flowers. Would students like to give Annie or Herman a present? Have students draw 10 things they would like to give Annie or Herman.

- Place a small, brown paper bag labeled "Herman's Bag" at a learning center or other work space. Fill the bag with 10 small rocks or marbles. Students can use the bag to practice counting to 10 and back; each time they take the rocks out of the bag, they must count backward; to put the rocks back into the bag, they must count forward.

CHAPTER 6

Riddle With Herman

Puppet Skit

About the Puppet Skit

"What am I thinking of?" Herman asks Annie as he pulls some objects out of his bag. Children take the role of Annie and play along with Herman's guessing game.

Key Concept

- Comparing measurements with words such as *shorter than* and *longer than*

Before Performing

- Photocopy the puppets and masks on pages 22-24.
- Copy the Riddle Rhyme and Annie's Refrain onto chart paper. Encourage children to join in as you chant the rhyme.
- You will need a bag for Herman to use in the riddle game. The bag must be large enough to hold several items (a paper lunch bag will work well). Place a crayon, pencil, and paintbrush in the bag. For this first telling of the play, make sure that the paintbrush is the longest of the three and that the crayon is the shortest.
- See page 5 for more tips on using the puppet skit.

Riddle Rhyme:

Annie, Annie, listen do.

I have a riddle just for you.

I'm thinking of something you can see.

It's longer than the crayon.

What do you think it could be?

Annie's Refrain:

Riddles, riddles, are fun to do.

Herman, Herman please give me a clue.

Extending the Skit

- Repeat the play, but this time have Herman think of the crayon or the pencil instead of the paintbrush. Adjust the riddle rhymes accordingly.
- Fill the bag with items that share different attributes so that other measures can be compared. For example, balls of modeling clay of different colors and sizes could initiate comparison of weight. The line in the rhyme, "Is it longer than the crayon?" will change depending on the attributes to be compared. For example, if you were to place different-sized balls of modeling clay in the bag, you would change the line to "Is it heavier than the yellow ball?"

Activity Guide ★ MATHmatazz 13

Riddle With Herman
Puppet Skit Script

As the skit begins, the teacher is in the front of the classroom holding a Herman puppet. Herman's bag sits nearby. It contains a crayon, pencil, and paintbrush.

Props
- a puppet for each child
- Herman's bag containing a crayon, pencil and paintbrush, all of different lengths

Characters

Herman: You will read the role of Herman.

Annie: Give an Annie puppet to each child in the class. Children can move their puppets as they say the rhyme, and indicate they have a response by raising their puppets.

Teacher: In the very beginning of the script, you will introduce the play as the narrator.

☞ This symbol points to italicized text, which will help you to prompt students to follow along with the action.

Teacher as Narrator: Today Herman is going to teach you—Annie, his very best friend—a fun riddle game. Here is Herman now.

☞ *Bring your Herman puppet to front center with a bag of the props mentioned in the preparation section.*

Teacher as Herman: Hi, Annie.

☞ *Prompt the children to wave their Annie puppets and to respond.*

Herman: Annie, I put together some fun things so we can play my newest and best riddle game.

☞ *Ask a volunteer prop person to help you empty the bag. Three children may come forward to hold the items so that they are visible to all.*

Herman: I have a crayon, a pencil, and a paintbrush. Annie, how are all the things in my bag alike?

☞ *Encourage children to suggest the sorting rule used. Children may suggest things we can draw with, things that roll etc. Then prompt the class to read Annie's riddle.*

Annie: Riddles, riddles, are fun to do.

Herman, Herman please give me a clue.

Herman: Annie, Annie, listen do.

I have a riddle just for you.

I'm thinking of something you can see.

It's longer than the crayon.

What do you think it could be?

☞ *Prompt children to respond. (Both the pencil and the paintbrush are longer than the crayon)*

Herman: **Hmm, you are right about that. It could be the pencil or the paintbrush. Time for you to ask a question to get another clue!**

Annie, here is what to do, if you want another clue.

Ask a question about what you see.

Use one of these words:

Long, longer, longest

Long, longer, longest

That's how to get another clue from me.

☞ *As you say "long, longer, longest," move your hands farther apart with each word to add meaning to the language. Invite children to join in. Then prompt the class to read Annie's rhyme.*

Annie: **Riddles, riddles are fun to do.**

Herman, Herman please give me a clue.

☞ *Encourage children to suggest questions that Herman could ask Annie. For example:* Is it longer than the pencil? Is it the longest thing in the collection? Is it as long as the pencil? *Respond to their questions by inserting the new clue in the rhyme.*

Herman: **I'm thinking of something you can see.**

It's longer than the crayon.

It's longer than the pencil.

What do you think it could be?

☞ *Encourage children to identify the item Herman is thinking of. You can have children compare the items and check whether they have, in fact, followed the two clues. In this case they would see whether the paintbrush is longer than the crayon as well as longer than the pencil.*

Herman: **Annie, you did it. You solved the riddle. Good for you! Do you want to play again? This time *you* can give the clues!**

☞ *Repeat the play, but this time prompt Annie to make Herman guess which item* she *is thinking of.*

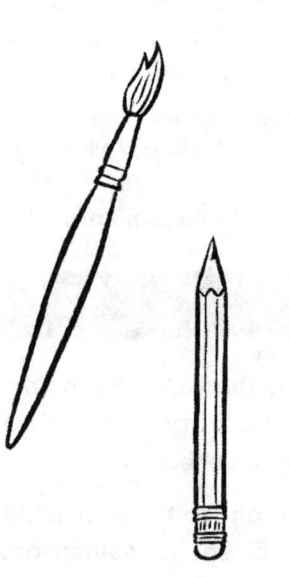

Shapes for Sale

Key Concepts

- Using names of two-dimensional shapes to describe three-dimensional solids
- Identifying solids including a *ball, box, cylinder, rectangular prism,* and *pyramid*

About the Video

Annie's Aunt Sally has a new job—she's a door-to-door shapes salesperson. But she's not sure how to sell all the balls, boxes, cylinders, prisms, and pyramids in her sales case. Leave it to Annie and Herman to help get Aunt Sally's sales pitch into super shape!

Approximate running time: 15 minutes

Before Viewing

- Annie's Aunt Sally is coming to visit in this show. Ask students to imagine and describe or draw a picture of what Aunt Sally will look like.
- Ask: *What do you have to know if you want to work in a store as a salesperson?*
- This video is all about shapes. Ask: *What is a shape?* Make an illustrated list of all of the shapes students can think of.
- Ask: *Which are two-dimensional* (flat) *and which are three-dimensional* (not flat)?
- Make the explanation more vivid with a demonstration. Bring in a styrofoam ball cut in half. Show the two halves together as a sphere and then show the half sphere—demonstrating that the cross-section of the sphere is a circle. Do the same with other shapes: the cross-section of a cylinder is a circle; of a rectangular prism (any rectangle-shaped solid box) is a rectangle, etc.
- See page 5 for more tips on using the videotape.

 **The Song**

In the song "It's Hip to Be Square," your students will learn about the properties of this four-sided shape.

Extending the Video

- Replay the video. Each time Aunt Sally takes a new shape out of her bag, pause the tape. Ask students to try to identify objects in the classroom that are of that shape. Keep a running list on the chalkboard.
- Fill an old suitcase or paper bag with objects of different shapes. Tell students that they will get to be shapes salespeople, just like Aunt Sally. Ask students, one at a time, to pull an object out of the bag, then "sell" or describe it to the class by using the vocabulary of shapes (*It has three sides; It has a circle on one end; etc.*).

CHAPTER 8

Animal Trouble

Book

Key Concepts

- Counting to 10
- Understanding ways to make numbers to 10

About the Book

In this counting book, students will count animals at the zoo along with Annie and Herman. But the friends are so busy counting that they don't notice that a mischievous monkey is setting the animals loose!

Before Reading

- Ask students to look at the book cover. Ask: *How many of you have been to the zoo?* With students, count the number of animals on the cover, and explain that in the book, Annie and Herman will count the animals in the zoo.

- Let students know that you'll be asking them to retell the story to each other after you've read it.

- Ask: *What kinds of animals might you see at the zoo? What kind of animals do you think you will see in this book?*

- Ask: *Which of the animals on the cover is the tallest? Which is the shortest? How many pink animals do you see on the cover?*

- Ask: *What do you think is the job of a zookeeper? Do you think counting is important for zookeepers? Why?*

- See page 5 for more tips on using the book.

Extending the Book

- To strengthen both language arts and math skills, put students in pairs or small groups, and ask them to retell the story to one another using words or pictures. If you wish, let students use their Annie and Herman puppets or masks (pp. 22 – 24).

- Turn to the back of the book for more extension activities.

CHAPTER 9

Story Time

Key Concepts

- Sequencing events in order of time
- Sequencing events involving money

About the Game

Students choose story cards featuring Annie and Herman in different situations and place the cards in sequence on the game board.

Before Playing

- Use this cooperative game for 1-3 players to reinforce concepts in Chapter 9.
- Read the rules together.
- Prompt students to talk about the game board. Ask: *Where will Annie's story cards go? Herman's? What other characters have a story to tell?*
- Introduce and discuss the story cards. Explain that there are five cards for each story. Once students have collected all five cards, they will put them in order and tell their story.
- See page 5 for more tips on using the game.

Preparation

- Remove the game board from the pocket in the back of this Activity Guide.
- On the back of the game board, you'll find a reproducible rule sheet, as well as reproducible story cards. Duplicate and cut out the cards. You may wish to color the cards, and/or laminate them for greater durability.

Extending the Game

- Have students make their own set of story cards.
- Ask children to act out the stories or use the character puppets to present their stories at a drama center.
- Ask children to draw a sixth story card for a character to show what they think might have happened next.

Bugs, Slugs and Butterflies

CHAPTER 10

Book

About the Book

How many bugs are there in Annie's garden? That's what Annie and Herman are trying to find out. There's only one problem: the creepy, crawly critters just won't sit still!

Key Concepts

- Understanding the concept of joining groups
- Understanding the concept of separating groups

Before Reading

- Ask students to look at the book cover. Ask: *Where are Annie and Herman? Do you have a garden at home? What kinds of bugs can you find in a garden?* Explain that in the book, Annie and Herman will add and subtract the number of bugs in their garden.

- Read the title of the book. Ask: *Do you know what a slug is? What do slugs look like? Are they fast or slow?*

- Do students think it would be easy or difficult to count bugs in a garden? Ask students to predict what they think might happen in the story. Ask: *Will Annie and Herman be able to count the bugs?*

- Let students know that you'll be asking them to retell the story to each other after you've read it.

- See page 5 for more tips on using the book.

Extending the Book

- To strengthen both language arts and math skills, put students in pairs or small groups, and ask them to retell the story to one another using words or pictures.

- Remind students of the predictions they made before reading. Ask: *Were Annie and Herman able to count all the bugs? What solution did they come up with?*

- In the back of the book, you'll find questions that get students to interact with the book and ideas for taking into the classroom what students have learned about pre-addition and subtraction from Annie and Herman.

CHAPTER 11: The Super-Duper Art Show

Key Concepts

- Counting numbers to 31
- Ordering numbers to 31
- Comparing numbers to 31
- Skip counting by 5s

About the Video

Annie can't wait to enter the local art contest. The flyer says, "Turn Junk Into Art," and she's making a necklace. But should she use 1–10 pieces of junk, 11–20 pieces, or 21–30 pieces? With Herman's help she'll make the most super-duper necklace ever!

Approximate running time: 12 minutes

Before Viewing

- Ask: *Have you ever entered a contest before? What did you have to make or do to enter?* In this video, Annie takes part in an art show. Explain that in an art show, people display things they make.

- For the art show, Annie must use recycled materials to make her entry. Ask: *Have you ever used junk to make something new?* Use this as an opportunity to talk about recycling and reusing.

- Explain that in this video, Annie and Herman will use skip counting. Review or introduce counting by 5s with the class. Challenge the class to skip count up to 30. Let them know that when Annie and Herman skip count in the video, students can count along with the characters.

- See page 5 for more tips on using the videotape.

 **The Song**

In the song "Skip Count," Annie and Herman count by 5s up to 30.

Extending the Video

- Hold your own Super-Duper Art Show. Provide students with lengths of yarn and an assortment of items that they can use to make a necklace: buttons, beads, empty spools of thread, paper clips, etc. Invite students to make necklaces, then count up the number of pieces of junk they used and determine which category they should enter: 1–10, 11–20, or 21–30. Or assign categories to students, and instruct them to create a necklace that fits that category.

- For a language arts activity, ask students to imagine what the giant was doing in Annie's backyard. Have them illustrate their explanations and present their stories to the rest of the class.

CHAPTER 12

The Mixed-Up Collection

Book

Key Concepts

- Adding to make sums up to 10

- Subtracting from groups of 10 or less

About the Book

Annie has a collection of 7 red things. Herman has a collection of 6 rocks. There's a lot of addition and subtraction in store when the two friends decide to trade items in their collections. By the time they're through, they'll end up with the most mixed-up collection ever!

Before Reading

- Ask students to look at the book cover. Ask: *How many balls are on the table? How many shells? How many balls and shells in all?* Explain that in this book, Annie and Herman will add and subtract as they trade items in their collections.

- Let students know that you'll be asking them to retell the story to each other after you've read it.

- Ask: *How many of you have collections?* Encourage students to describe the kinds of things in their collections. What kinds of things do they think Annie and Herman might collect?

- Explain that in the story, Annie and Herman share the items in their collections. Use this as a springboard to a discussion about sharing. Ask: *Do you share things with your friends and classmates? How does sharing make you feel?*

- See page 5 for more tips on using the book.

Extending the Book

- To strengthen both language arts and math skills, put students in pairs or small groups, and ask students to retell the story to one another using words or pictures.

- In the back of the book, you'll find questions that get students to interact with the book as well as ideas for taking into the classroom what students have learned about addition and subtraction from Annie and Herman.

Pencil Puppet Templates
Annie and Herman

Annie

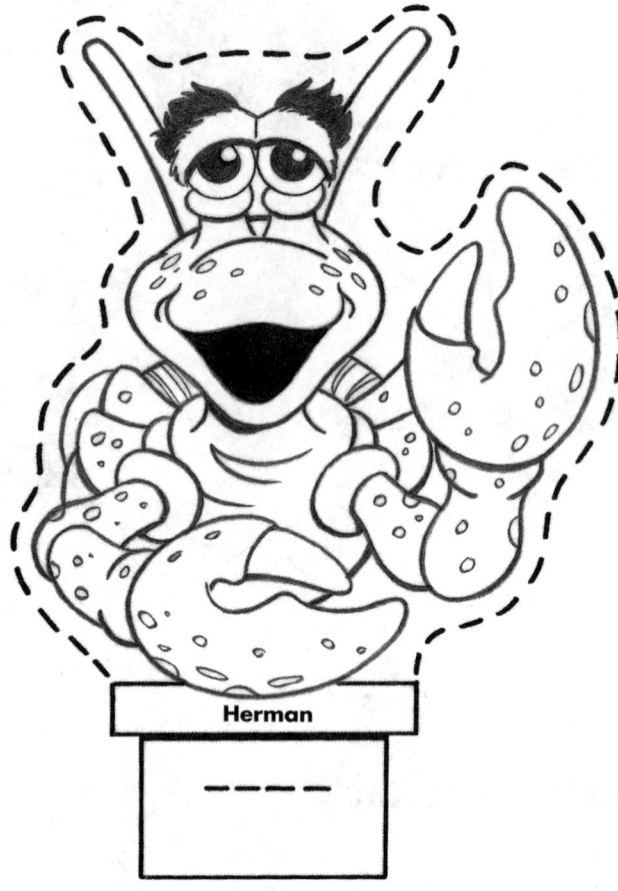

Herman

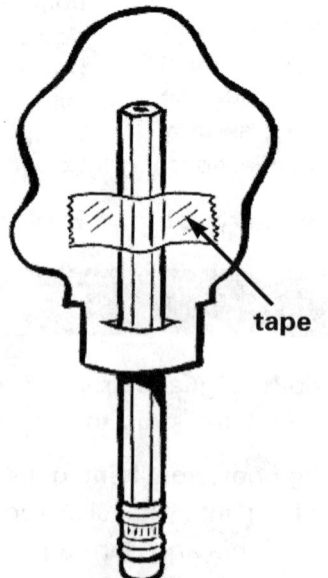

tape

Photocopy enough puppets for each student in your class. Instruct students to color in their puppets and to cut on the dotted lines. Cut a slit along the dotted lines in the base of each puppet. Slide the top of a pencil through the slit. Then tape the pencil top to the back of the puppet, as shown.

Photocopy one mask for each "Annie" in your class. Instruct students to color and cut out masks along the dashed lines. Follow the dashed lines to cut holes for students' eyes. Punch a small hole on each side of the mask. Tie a 10" piece of string to each hole. To wear masks, tie strings together.

Photocopy one mask for each "Herman" in your class. Instruct students to color and cut out masks along the dashed lines. Follow the dashed lines to cut holes for students' eyes. Punch a small hole on each side of the mask. Tie a 10" piece of string to each hole. To wear masks, tie strings together.

24 MATHmatazz Activity Guide